CW00734691

SPIRIT OF

EDINBURGH

JASON FRIEND

First published in Great Britain in 2010

British Library Cataloguing-in-Publication Data
A CIP record for this title is available from the British Library

ISBN 978 0 85710 010 8

PiXZ Books
Halsgrove House, Ryelands Industrial Estate,
Bagley Road, Wellington, Somerset TA21 9PZ
Tel: 01823 653777
Fax: 01823 216796
email: sales@halsgrove.com

An imprint of Halstar Ltd, part of the Halsgrove group of companies
Information on all Halsgrove titles is available at: www.halsgrove.com

Printed and bound in China by Toppan Leefung Printing Ltd

Introduction

Edinburgh is the picturesque capital city of Scotland. Revered by tourists and locals alike, the features of the city are considered so unique that they have been protected for future generations by the awarding of 'World Heritage status'.

Essentially Edinburgh is two towns, which have amalgamated to create a sprawling mixture of ancient and modern architecture that spreads from the heart of the city. The castle is situated upon Castle Rock, which has dominated the skyline ever since it was used as a stronghold in the times of the Iron Age when a fort originally sat high on this ancient volcanic plug.

The Old Town maintains the charms of its medieval roots and boasts a number of historic buildings to be found alongside the spine road of the Royal Mile, which links the Royal Palace of Holyroodhouse with the castle. From here steep roads and narrow alleyways form a web of historic locations for the visitor to explore. In complete contrast to the chaotic design of the Old Town, the organised structure of the New Town is home to some fine architecture including the buildings of Charlotte Square, considered by many to be one of the finest Georgian squares in the world.

Within the pages of this book, I hope to share with you some of the reasons why this city is considered amongst the most spectacular cities in the United Kingdom, and indeed Europe. This book is a photographic record of my quest to discover the true spirit of Edinburgh.

Acknowledgements

A huge thank you to the people of Edinburgh who have approached me as I marched around the city, tripod in hand, and have shown great interest in the project. An extra special thank you to Vicky and Fanis for their wonderful inside city knowledge and for initially showing me some of the viewpoints photographed within this book.

Thank you once more to Steven Pugsley and the rest of the team at Halsgrove for making this book a reality.

The support of family and friends is important when I am working on a book so I would like to wholeheartedly thank all of you including John Friend, Penny, Roy and Mark Whitehouse and Valerie Hodgkins. A big 'Thumbs up' to Robert Mitchell who always loves to hear of my adventures in his Scottish Homelands.

As ever my wife Lynette has been there to support and encourage me whenever I have needed it most, and my baby boy Rhys has provided me with numerous reasons to smile, which always makes the undertaking of a project far more enjoyable.

Opposite page:
The Dugald Stewart Monument on Calton Hill, looking
towards the Castle and the Old Town of Edinburgh.

Originally the townhouse of the old Laird of Cockpen, this building was to become known as the Outlook Tower before its present title of the Camera Obscura.

Opposite page:
Looking towards the George Heriot's School on Lauriston Place in the Old Town, from the Castle Esplanade.

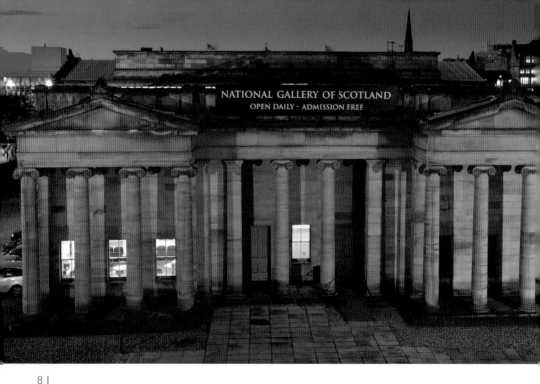

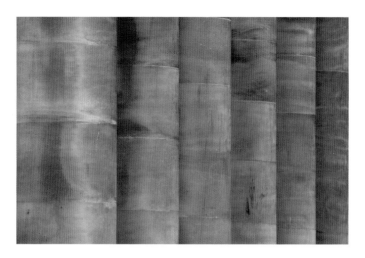

Detail of the pillars which are typical of the grand architecture
of the National Gallery of Scotland.

Opposite page:
The National Gallery of Scotland building viewed at dusk.

Statue of the Duke of Wellington on horseback
situated in the front of the Register House.

Opposite page:
Erected in 1823 in honour of Henry Dundas, the Melville Monument stands proud
in St Andrew's Square. The statue depicts Dundas looking towards George Street.

Johnston Terrace Wildlife Reserve, a Scottish Wildlife Trust walled wildlife garden in the centre of Edinburgh.

Opposite page:
Trees and grass lawn in Princes Street Gardens, created in the 1820s when the Nor Loch was drained.

St Anthony's Chapel high above
St Margaret's Loch, viewed from
the Salisbury Crags.

Opposite page:
The Palace of Holyroodhouse, the
official residence in Scotland of
Her Majesty the Queen.

Looking down on the cobble
road of West Bow, near the
Grassmarket in the Old Town

The New College and Assembly Hall on The Mound were opened in 1846 as the Free Church of Scotland New College. More recently the Assembly Hall has been used as a debating chamber for the Scottish Parliament prior to the construction of the new Parliament Building at Holyrood.

Statue of Greyfriars Bobby, the famous loyal Skye Terrier who la[] on the grave of his master John G[] for 14 years after his death in 185[] only leaving the grave briefly to find food.

Opposite page:
The grand architecture of Castle[] Hill School, opened in 1889, loca[] on the south side of Castle Hill.

John Knox House on the Royal Mile.
John Knox, whom Mary Queens of Scots
believed to be the most dangerous
man in her Kingdom, is thought to have
lived in this house in Netherbow
for the last few months of his life.

Opposite page:
African Woman and Child sculpture,
a commissioned piece of work by
Scottish sculptor and artist Anne Davidson,
located on the corner of Festival Square
and Lothian Road.

Frontage of a church along
the Georgian Calton Terraces,
designed by William Henry Playfa

Opposite page:
Georgian house located on
the north side of Charlotte
Square in the New Town.

Firth of Forth.

Opposite page:
Looking across Edinburgh
New Town.

The Edinburgh Playhouse, originally opened as a cinema in 1929, was designed by architect John Fairweather who gained inspiration for the design from the Roxy Theatre in New York.

Opposite page:
New Uberior House, a modern construction on the edge of the financial district.

Canal boats moored in the
Lochrin Basin near Fountainbridge.
Now known as the Edinburgh Quay,
the site has seen recent redevelopment
and a number of bars and apartments
are situated along the quayside.

Opposite page:
Traditional buildings reflected in
the windows of modern architecture.

Ferris wheel alongside the monument to Sir Walter Scott.

Opposite page:
Monument to Adam Smith opposite the Edinburgh City Chambers on the Royal Mile.

Nelson's Monument located
Calton Hill, erected to celebra
Nelson's victory at the
Battle of Trafalgar in 1805.

Opposite page:
The National Monument on
Calton Hill, known by many c
Edinburgh's Disgrace, funds f
its completion having run out sh
after construction started in 18

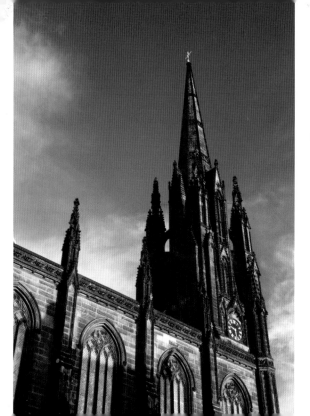

The Hub, originally known as the
Assembly Hall, a historic landmark
of the Royal Mile and a Grade
A listed building constructed between
1842 and 1845.

Opposite page:
Holyrood Park, part of the
Holyroodhouse complex, a
local recreational area for the
residents of the city.

The Queen's Gallery, originally built as the Holyrood Free Church, which forms part of the Palace of Holyroodhouse complex.

Despite the modern glass façade of the Festival Theatre, it is actually Edinburghs' longest continuous theatre site with a theatre being located here since 1830.

A creeper clinging to a wall of a residential house in the New Town.

Opposite page:
The foundations for the Gothic-style Church of St John the Evangelist were laid in March 1816, with the building finally consecrated in 1818.

Public footpath running through an avenue of trees in the Meadows, a large expanse of open greenery found near the centre of the city.

Opposite page:
Cobbled alleyway near the historic Grassmarket.

Ross Fountain was cast in France in the early 1860s befo being exhibited in the Grea Exhibition (London) in 1862 a finally being installed in its pres home of the West Princes Stre Gardens some ten years late

Opposite page:
Statue of Field Marshal Earl Haig located on the Edinburg Castle Esplanade.

Balmoral Hotel clock tower, often referred to as the most photographed clock tower in Scotland.

Opposite page:
The Scotsman building alongside the North Bridge, linking Princes Street with the Edinburgh Old Town.

Milne's Court, a narrow passageway
heading to the Royal Mile.

Opposite page:
Cobbled pedestrian walkway on the
Leith Commercial Quay.

47

Monument to Sir Walter Scott known simply as 'Scott's Monument' located along the busy Princes Street.

Opposite page:
Edinburgh Castle dominates the Edinburgh skyline as a result of its elevated position on Castle Rock.

Florentine-style central dome on the Royal Bank of Scotland building located on The Mound. Inspired by the seventeenth-century Italian painter and architect, Pietro da Cortona, the dome was topped by a statue of the Greek god, Victory, by sculptor John Rhind.

Opposite page:
Thomas Hamilton's obelisk and Governor's House located on Calton Hill.

Above and opposite page:
Typical architecture of the shops and offices located along the busy Princes Street.

Canongate Kirk, built in 1691
by Scottish architect James Smith,
is located in Canongate which was
a separate burgh before becoming
part of the City of Edinburgh in 1856

Opposite page:
Greyfriars Kirk was completed in
1620 making it one of the oldest
surviving buildings outside of
the Old Town.

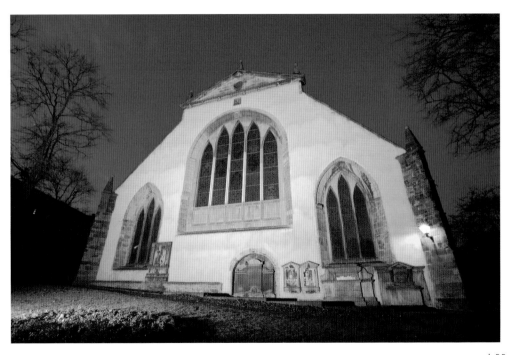

Grand house with whitewashed walls, located near the Castle Esplanade.

Opposite page:
Birds flock around Saint Cuthbert's Parish Church
and the Gothic-style Church of St John the Evangelist.

Courtyard viewed from the
George IV Bridge, which was constructed
to link the Old and New Towns.

Opposite page:
A prominent feature of the Edinburgh
skyline, the Bank of Scotland head office on
The Mound. Construction of this impressive
building was completed in 1806.

Home of the Scottish Parliament, the design of the Holyrood Building was described as "growing out of the land" by architect Enric Miralles.

Opposite page:
Looking south from Castle Hill across the city towards the Pentland Hills.

View overlooking the Old Town situated alongside
the extinct volcano known as Arthur's Seat.

Opposite page:
The Dean Gallery, part of the National Galleries of Scotland, opened in 1999
although the building was originally an orphanage designed by Thomas Hamilton.

Edinburgh Castle is built upon the remains of an extinct volcano.
Originally known as Lookout Hill but now known as Castle Rock,
it has been used as a stronghold for over 3000 years.